A Tribute to
THE YOUNG AT HEART

L. Frank Baum

By Jill C. Wheeler

Published by Abdo & Daughters, 4940 Viking Drive, Suite 622, Edina, Minnesota 55435.

Copyright © 1997 by Abdo Consulting Group, Inc., Pentagon Tower, P.O. Box 36036, Minneapolis, Minnesota 55435 USA. International copyrights reserved in all countries. No part of this book may be reproduced in any form without written permission from the publisher.

Printed in the United States.

Cover and Interior Photo credits: Bettmann Film Archive
Wide World Photos

Edited by Julie Berg

Library of Congress Cataloging-in-Publication Data

Wheeler, Jill, C., 1964—
    L. Frank Baum / Jill C. Wheeler.
        p. cm. -- (A tribute to the Young at Heart)
    Includes index.
    Summary: A brief biography of the author of the well-known children's classic, "The Wizard of Oz."
    ISBN 1-56239-787-7
    1. Baum, L. Frank (Lyman Frank), 1856-1919 -- Biography--Juvenile literature.
    2. Authors, American--20th century--Biography--juvenile literature. [1. Baum, L. Frank (Lyman Frank), 1856-1919. 2. Authors, American.] I. Title. II. Series: Tribute to the Young at Heart.
    PS3503.A923Z93   1997
    813'.4--dc21   96-29791
    [B]   CIP
                                     AC

Contents

ALWAYS TELLING STORIES

Maud Gage Baum looked around the store impatiently. Where was Frank? she wondered. Her eyes scanned the store. She saw counters lined with tableware and glassware. She saw lamps, baskets, and toys. She saw everything but her husband.

Suddenly, she heard peals of childish laughter from the wooden sidewalk outside the store. She walked briskly to the door of Baum's Bazaar in Aberdeen, South Dakota. There was her husband, Frank. He was telling stories again to a group of local children.

Frank was always telling stories, and he did it well. In the late 1880s, stories were a major type of entertainment. There was no television or radio. Not everyone had access to many books. Instead, they relied on telling stories or playing games, or just talking.

Lyman Frank Baum was never at a loss for a story. Throughout his life, he used his vivid imagination to weave tales. Most were fantasy stories or modern fairy tales. Some were mysteries. Some were thrillers. Many of them found their way to paper. From there, they became books.

Frank Baum wrote more than 60 books during his career. His most famous work is *The Wonderful Wizard Of Oz*. Seventy years after Frank wrote the book, it had become one of the 15 best-selling books of the 20th century. It has been adapted for the stage and the screen. The 1939 movie "The Wizard of Oz" starring Judy Garland has become a film classic known to almost everyone.

While Frank is best-known for creating the fanciful world of Oz, his career included many highlights. He worked as a journalist and a salesman. He raised purebred chickens. He even acted for a while. No matter what he did, he brought laughter to the lives of everyone around him.

A scene from *The Wizard of Oz.*

A SICKLY CHILDHOOD

Lyman Frank Baum was one of nine children born to Benjamin Baum and Cynthia Stanton Baum. From his birth on May 15, 1856, he was a sickly child. He had been born with a condition called angina pectoris. People with this ailment often get chest pains because their hearts don't get enough oxygen.

Frank's parents worried about him. They wouldn't let him play roughly. They were afraid his weak heart couldn't take it. They even hired private tutors to teach their children in their home near Syracuse, New York. Frank grew up as a shy boy who loved to read and preferred to be alone. He invented fantasies to entertain himself. Sometimes he invented funny voices for his toys. Other times he created imaginary playmates.

Frank read fantasy stories whenever he could. However, he didn't like fairy tales. "One thing I never liked then . . . was the introduction of witches and goblins into the story," he recalled. "I didn't like the little dwarfs in the woods bobbing up with their horrors." Scarecrows also frightened him. He often dreamt of them coming to life and chasing him. These fears made Frank determined to write his own fairy tale someday.

When Frank was 12, his parents decided he was well enough to go away to school. He spent two years at Peekskill Academy. It is a military school in New York. He hated the school and was glad to return home. Shortly after he got back, his father gave him a special present. It was a printing press.

Frank always had an interest in writing and publishing. With his new press, he could do just that. He and his brother created a neighborhood newspaper. They called it *The Rose Lawn Home Journal*. They wrote verses, articles, and stories for their paper. They even sold advertisements in it. Between editions, Frank and his brother printed stationery, signs, and programs.

Soon it was time to buy a bigger printing press. Frank did, and began to publish a literary magazine. He called it *The Empire*. He also published a magazine about stamp collecting. Stamp collecting was one of his hobbies. Another hobby was raising a special breed of chickens called

Hamburgs. Frank got into the chicken business in his late teens and started a magazine for poultry enthusiasts. He called it *The Poultry Record*. Later he would write a book about raising chickens called *The Book of the Hamburgs*.

The creator of *The Wizard of Oz*, L. Frank Baum (1856-1919).

BITTEN BY THE ACTING BUG

Frank went through many jobs in his late teens and early twenties. He was lucky his parents were wealthy. His father had made a lot of money in the oil business. The money helped him support Frank while he tried his hand at different jobs. For a while, Frank worked as a salesman for his father. In 1877, he started a newspaper in Pennsylvania called *The New Era*.

None of his jobs lasted very long. Frank always found something else that he wanted to do. When he was 23, he decided to pursue acting. He had acted a little when he was a teenager. This time he joined the Albert M. Palmer's Union Square Theatre in New York as a professional actor.

A year later, he began managing a chain of opera houses his father owned. The opera houses featured plays and musicals. Frank organized his own acting company to put on some of Shakespeare's plays. He recalled one time when he was doing a performance of Hamlet on a rickety stage. The actor playing the ghost tripped and fell through the stage boards. The audience thought that was supposed to happen and applauded wildly. They made the actors repeat the stunt five times.

Eventually Frank began to write plays, too. One of his plays became quite successful. He entitled it *The Maid of Arran*. In addition to writing it, Frank produced it, directed it, and starred in it as the leading role. The show was so popular Frank and his company took it on the road to play in other cities.

When he wasn't on stage, Frank had other business on his mind. While writing his play, he had met a young woman named Maud Gage. Frank made frequent trips to visit her in the summer of 1882. Finally, he asked her to marry him. She agreed and told him to wait while she asked her mother.

Frank loved to tell the story of what he heard then. "I heard Mrs. Gage say, 'I won't have my daughter be a darned fool and marry an actor.'" Maud replied that in that case, she was saying good-bye. She said she was going to marry Frank. She said she assumed her mother wouldn't want a darned fool around the house.

Mrs. Gage finally agreed to the marriage. It took place at Maud's home in Fayetteville, New York, on November 9, 1882. Frank continued to travel and act until Maud became pregnant with their first child. Then he wrote and staged several other plays. None was as successful as *The Maid of Arran*. He also worked as a traveling salesman for his father's company. The company, called Baum's Castorine, made axle grease.

Opposite page: This is a studio portrait of L. Frank Baum. Baum would write his stories in long hand then type them out with two fingers on a typewriter.

DAKOTA TERRITORY

Frank and Maud's first child, Frank Jr., was born in 1883. His brother, Robert, arrived in 1886. Frank was still running Baum's Castorine. A year later, his father died. Shortly after that, Frank went to work one day to find the company clerk shot dead in the office. He discovered the man had killed himself after losing the firm's money to gambling.

Suddenly Frank found himself with a bankrupt company. His opera houses also had failed. He decided it was time for a new beginning.

In those days, everyone was talking about Dakota Territory. That's the land now called North and South Dakota. Prospectors had discovered gold in Dakota Territory and everyone wanted to get in on the action. Three of Maud's siblings already had moved west to try their fortunes in the new land. Frank and Maud decided to follow.

The Baum family settled in a town called Aberdeen. Later, it would be in the state of South Dakota. Frank rented a house for his family and rented a store to run. He called it Baum's Bazaar. The family began to enjoy the whirlwind social life of their new town. Maud gave birth to their third son, Harry, in December 1889.

By that time, two years of bad weather had ruined the local crops. The people who visited Baum's Bazaar had no money to pay for their purchases. The store failed. Frank took a job running *The Aberdeen Saturday Pioneer*, a weekly newspaper. He did most of the writing, as well as the printing.

Sadly, Frank lost his newspaper to bankruptcy two years later. "I decided the sheriff wanted the paper more than I did," he recalled. Frank packed up his family, which now included a fourth son, Kenneth. They moved to Chicago.

The man who created the Land of Oz, L. Frank Baum, with a group of children around 1912.

A WRITING LIFE

Chicago was a bustling young city in May 1891. Frank arrived as the city prepared to host the World's Fair. He took a job as a reporter with the *Evening Post*. He earned just $20 per week. He took another job selling china and glassware after the newspaper cut his wages. He had no idea how much china he was supposed to sell. So he sold as much as he could. He surprised everyone with how well he did.

Frank noticed many things as he traveled from store to store. He thought the store owners could do a better job of displaying their wares. Once he helped design a window. He used a wash boiler, stovepipe, and a saucepan to make a metal person. He gave them a funnel for a hat. The funny looking fellow became Baum's model for the Tin Woodman in "The Wizard of Oz."

All the while, Baum delighted his sons with stories. Yet when he told them fairy tales, they often had questions. They wanted to know how a cow could jump over a moon, for example. He decided to answer their questions in a book. He worked with a local illustrator to produce *Mother Goose in Prose*. The book was published in 1897 and became an instant success. The money from *Mother Goose* allowed Frank to quit his job as a traveling salesman. He settled down to write and publish a magazine, *The Show Window*. The magazine helped store owners make their window displays more attractive. Doing the magazine also was easier on Frank's frail heart than being a salesman. He also wrote a book on the subject of window dressing.

Frank soon became involved with the Chicago Press Club. There he met an illustrator named William Denslow. William drew some illustrations for a book of poetry Frank had written. The two began talking about other projects as well. Frank showed him some of the children's verses he had scribbled on scraps of paper while traveling as a salesman. William agreed to illustrate the verses.

Frank typed up his poems for the new book. He used just two fingers when he typed. William made a drawing for each verse. Then they showed their work to a publisher. At first, no one wanted the book. William wanted the publisher to print all the drawings in color. No one printed each page in color in those days. Publishers found it too expensive. Eventually, Frank and William convinced the Hill Company to publish their book. *Father Goose, His Book* came out in September 1899. It went on to be the best-selling children's book of the year.

THE BIRTH OF OZ

Frank used his profits from *Father Goose* to buy a new home for his family. Then he and William began work on a new project. For years, Frank had been piecing a fairy tale together in his head. He tested it on his children. They loved it. Years later he talked about it.

"I was sitting on a hat rack in the hall, telling the kids a story. Suddenly this one moved right in and took possession. I shooed the children away and grabbed a piece of paper that was lying there on the rack and began to write. It really seemed to write itself. Then I couldn't find any regular paper. So I took anything at all, even a bunch of old envelopes."

Eventually Frank typed up his hand-written notes. The fairy tale became a manuscript. It was about a six-year-old girl named Dorothy who lived in Kansas. One day a tornado blew her to a magical land of strange creatures. Frank called it the land of Oz. There, Dorothy met a living Scarecrow. She met a Tin Woodman and a Cowardly Lion. Her new friends agreed to help her get back home to Kansas. They sought the help of a wonderful wizard to get Dorothy back home. On the way they met a wicked witch.

Frank liked to tell lots of different stories about how he came up with the idea for the book. He even told some people that he got the name Oz from his file cabinet. One drawer was labeled A-G. Another was labeled H-N. The third was labeled O-Z.

William drew more than 100 illustrations to accompany Frank's fairy tale. He and Frank wanted to call the book The Emerald City. Then they learned of a strange superstition in the publishing world. Many publishers believe any book with the name of a jewel in the title will fail. So they changed the name to *The Wonderful Wizard of Oz*. Once again, they insisted that the publisher use color illustrations throughout the book.

The Wonderful Wizard of Oz hit bookstores in September 1900. It cost just $1.50. It became the best-selling children's book of the year.

Later that year Frank needed money. His wife suggested he ask his publisher for an advance. An advance is money paid to an author for books that have not yet been sold. Frank shyly asked for $100. His publisher said instead, they would pay Frank for all the books they had sold to date. He gave Frank a check for more than $3,400!

OZ HITS THE STAGE

Today, many popular books quickly become movies. Yet movies barely existed in 1900. Instead, people often turned popular books into stage shows. That's exactly what Frank and William did with *The Wonderful Wizard of Oz*.

After writing another fantasy adventure called *Dot and Tot of Merryland*, they brought Oz to the stage. They worked with a composer to set the Oz story to music. In the process they changed the story. Frank had written it as a fantasy. It was hard to bring some of those elements to life, so they changed them. Instead, they focused more on the characters. Dorothy became a young woman instead of a girl. They also added new characters.

The final show included singing, dancing, and comedy acts. It opened in Chicago. Audiences loved it. Frank was amazed. He had never seen his imagination literally brought to life. "When the Scarecrow came to life on the first night . . . I expected strange sensations of wonder and awe," Frank said. "The appearance of the Tin Woodman made me catch my breath." He added that when he saw the field of human poppy flowers, he thought it was more real than his fondest dreams.

The Oz show moved on to New York. Touring companies took the show to stages around the nation. It played, on and off, for nine years. All the while Frank kept writing. He wrote new children's books like *A New Wonderland*, *American Fairy Tales*, *The Army Alphabet,* and *The Navy Alphabet*. He wrote a science fiction novel for teenagers called *The Master Key: An Electrical Fairy Tale*. He dedicated the book to his son Rob, who loved science and experimenting. None of the books were as popular as *Oz*.

All the while, hundreds of Frank's young fans sent him letters. They wanted more Oz. "I began to receive letters from children," Frank recalled. "[They asked] me to write 'something more' about the Scarecrow and the Tin Woodman."

Frank wrote to one little girl that he would write more about Oz after a thousand children sent him a thousand letters. Sure enough, he received more than one thousand letters. He kept his promise. He published *The Marvelous Land of Oz* in 1904.

NEW CHARACTERS, NEW ADVENTURES

The new Oz book did not include Dorothy. Frank wanted her story to be complete in the first book. With this book he introduced Tip. Tip joins the Scarecrow and Tin Woodman for a series of adventures. Along the way readers meet more new characters. These include a witch called Mombi, Jack Pumpkinhead, the Saw-Horse, and the Woggle-Bug.

Readers loved the new characters, especially the Woggle-Bug. Frank featured the Bug in a comic page he wrote for Sunday newspapers. Each week the comic included a riddle called "What Did the Woggle-Bug Say?" People could write in answers to the riddle and win money. It was a very popular contest.

Frank was a wealthy man by this time. He and his family had several homes around the country. They also began to travel a lot. They spent several years traveling and living in the American Southwest. Frank continued to write more books during this time. He wrote *The Woggle-Bug Book* and *Queen Zixi of Ix* for children. He also wrote an adult novel titled *The*

Fate of a Crown. He began a successful series of books for teenage girls called *Aunt Jane's Nieces*. He wrote them under the name of Edith Van Dyne.

In 1906, he took his family on a trip to Europe and Africa. The same year he published another children's book called *John Dough and the Cherub*. It was about a gingerbread man and the world's first incubator baby. Frank's funny characters kept people entertained. His imagination amazed them.

"I, too, like to hear about my funny creatures," he said. "I never know what strange characters are going to pop into my head when I begin telling a story. You know, I think up things for them to do. But when I start telling the story to the children, these characters seem to develop a life of their own. They often surprise me by that—just like living people."

Frank called on his imagination to write the third Oz book, *Ozma of Oz*. He brought back Dorothy due to his readers' demands. He introduced Billina, a talking hen, a mechanical man named Tik-Tok. He gave readers a new villain, the wicked Nome King.

Next he wrote *Dorothy and the Wizard in Oz* in 1906. Frank

worked on another stage adaptation of the Oz story for children. This time he was the star. He called the show "Fairylogue and the Radio-Plays." The show toured the nation. Yet the project was very expensive. Frank paid for everything himself. He had no money left when the show closed in 1908.

A scene from the musical *The Wizard of Oz.*

ON TO HOLLYWOOD

It wasn't the first time Frank had been broke. Yet he knew just what to do. He wrote more Oz books. Many parents now expected to give their children a new Oz book each Christmas.

Frank didn't disappoint them. *The Road to Oz* hit bookstores in 1909. In 1910 he published *The Emerald City of Oz*. He had decided he could ignore superstitions about using a jewel in the title. He also hoped it would be the last Oz book he ever would write. After the book came out, Frank and his family moved to Hollywood, California. Frank called their new home there Ozcot. Despite his popular books, he declared bankruptcy in 1911.

In 1912 he wrote *Sky Island*. He thought it was the best work he ever did. Sadly, people didn't want to read it. They only wanted more Oz. Frank gave them what they wanted with *The Patchwork Girl of Oz* in 1913.

Next, Frank turned back to the theater. On March 31, 1913, a new Oz musical opened in Los Angeles. Audiences loved "The Tik-Tok Man of Oz." It had dazzling special effects. The characters crossed a bridge that looked just like a shimmering rainbow. They also found a cavern filled with huge jewels. Lights inside the jewels made them sparkle brilliantly.

Even though people liked the show, it closed that summer. Back in California, Frank was hearing more and more about a new type of show. It was called a motion picture. Frank met many people who were working on these pictures. He and several others formed a new company. They called it the Oz Film Manufacturing Company.

The first book they filmed was *The Patchwork Girl of Oz*. It took them a month to film the five-reel, feature-length film. Next, the Oz Film Company completed a movie based on *Queen Zixi of Ix*. Their third film was "His Majesty, the Scarecrow of Oz." The movie had a cast of 130 people. It cost more than $23,500 to make. Back then, that was a lot of money.

Frank used some of the ideas in this third movie to write another Oz book. He called it *The Scarecrow of Oz*. It was published in 1915.

Opposite page: Scenes from the Hollywood production, *The Wizard of Oz*.

Frank's newest Oz book was a success. Sadly, his movies were not. Most people said only children would want to watch them. Some of the adults who saw them asked for their money back. No company was willing to distribute the films to movie theaters across the country.

Frank and his company made two more movies for adults. Both failed. After that, they decided to sell their movie studio. Universal Studios bought it.

THE FINAL CHAPTER

Frank was not even 60 years old when World War I began in 1914. The war seemed far away in Europe. Most Americans were still too busy worrying about their own lives to care about it.

In the Baum household, Frank's family worried about him. His health continued to get worse. His gallbladder caused him much pain. He also suffered from uncontrollable spasms in his face. Sometimes the paper he wrote on would be wet from his own tears. His health even forced him to give up writing for a while.

When he began writing again, he wrote *Rinkitink in Oz*. The book came out in 1916. The following year he wrote *The Lost Princess of Oz*. He was in terrible pain the whole time he was writing the book. He also was secretly writing two other books. He called them *The Magic of Oz* and *Glinda of Oz*. He hid them in a safe deposit box. He considered them his insurance. If he died, his family could have them published to earn money.

Frank finally agreed to let doctors operate on him. They removed his gallbladder. He was never the same after the surgery. He had to stay in bed all day because of his weak heart. Yet Frank refused to give up. He wrote *The Tin Woodman of Oz* while lying in bed. Parents were buying that book for their children in 1918.

The same year Frank took *The Magic of Oz* from his safe deposit box. He worked to get it ready for publication. He dedicated the book to the children of the soldiers fighting in World War I. America had joined in the war the year before.

Frank lived to see the end of World War I in fall 1918. Yet the following May, he suffered a stroke. One of the last things Frank told his wife was that the money from his books would sustain their family.

Frank died on May 6, 1919. Shortly after his death, *The Magic of Oz* appeared in bookstores. Maud Baum had *Glinda of Oz* published in 1920. She also agreed to let Frank's publisher find someone new to continue the Oz series. When the feature film "The Wizard of Oz" opened in August 1939, Maud was there to see it.

Today, more people have seen "The Wizard of Oz" than any

other movie in the world. It continues to be a popular movie on TV. In 1989, the Library of Congress named the movie a national treasure. In bookstores around the world, children still buy Oz books. No doubt, Frank Baum would be happy to know the legacy he created.

"When I was young I longed to write a great novel that should win me fame," he once said. "I have learned to regard fame as a will-o-the-wisp which, when caught, is not worth the possession. But to please a child is a sweet and lovely thing . . . I hope my book will succeed in that way—that the children will like it."

WRITINGS

Following are just a few of Frank Baum's many books. Read one to find out how a master storyteller spins a tale.

Mother Goose in Prose, 1897
Father Goose, His Book, 1899
The Wonderful Wizard of Oz, 1900
American Fairy Tales, 1901

Dot and Tot of Merryland, 1901

The Marvelous Land of Oz, 1904

Queen Zixi of Ix, 1905

Aunt Jane's Nieces, 1906

Aunt Jane's Nieces Abroad, 1906

Ozma of Oz, 1907

Dorothy and the Wizard in Oz, 1908

The Road to Oz, 1909

The Emerald City of Oz, 1910

The Sea Fairies, 1911

Sky Island, 1912

The Patchwork Girl of Oz, 1913

Tik-Tok of Oz, 1914

Aunt Jane's Nieces in the Red Cross, 1915

The Scarecrow of Oz, 1915

Rinkitink in Oz, 1916

The Lost Princess of Oz, 1917

The Tin Woodman of Oz, 1918

The Magic of Oz, 1919

Glinda of Oz, 1920

GLOSSARY OF TERMS

Advance — money paid to an author before his or her books are sold.

Angina pectoris — a condition where a person's heart doesn't get enough oxygen. It causes chest pains.

Bankrupt — having almost no money and/or possessions.

Gallbladder — a part of a person's body located near the liver.

Incubator — a machine that mimics the conditions needed for a living thing to grow.

Manuscript — the text of a book before it is published.

Stroke — When a blood vessel bursts in a person's brain.

Tutor — a private teacher.

INDEX